Knock on a Door

by Mary Thornton Blanton
illustrated by
Gwen Connelly

Published by The Dandelion House
A Division of The Child's World

for distribution by _____
BOOKS a division of SP Publications, Inc.
WHEATON. ILLINOIS 60187

Offices also in
Whitby, Ontario, Canada
Amersham-on-the-Hill, Bucks, England

Published by The Dandelion House, A Division of The Child's World, Inc.
© 1984 SP Publications, Inc. All rights reserved. Printed in U.S.A.

A Book for Preschoolers.

Library of Congress Cataloging in Publication Data

Blanton, Mary Thornton, 1926-
  Knock on a door.

  Summary: Explains how important it is to let
people all over the world know that Jesus loves and
cares for us all.
  1. Missions—Juvenile literature.   2. Witness
bearing (Christianity)—Juvenile literature.
[1. Missions.   2. Christian life]   I. Connelly,
Gwen, ill.   II. Title.
BV2065.B64   1984   266   84-7027
ISBN 0-89693-224-9

  1 2 3 4 5 6 7 8 9 10 11 12 R 90 89 88 87 86 85 84

Knock on a Door

Sunday School
4's and 5's

Let's play a game
and pretend to go
around the world
in a minute or so!

Let's pretend to visit children
  far away.
We'll tell them of Jesus
  and His love today.
Spin the arrow. . .one, two,
  three, four!

Look where we've landed.
Let's knock on the door.

"Wait! Please! Don't run away.
We've come to tell you of Jesus
    today."

They come. They smile.
"Hi, friends," we say.
"Let's talk about Jesus
while we play."

We make an igloo with cold,
    wet snow
as we talk of something special
    we know.
"Whether we are big or small,
Jesus loves us—one and all.

God made me.
God made you.

He made huskies . . .

seals . . .

and polar bears too."

9

Back to our room.
Spin the arrow once more.

Now look where we've landed.
Let's knock on the door.

"Hi, friends," we say.
"We've come from our church
    far, far away . . .
to tell you the Good News of
    Jesus today."

"Who is Jesus?" they want to know.
We say, "He's God's Son who was born
   long ago.
He was born in Bethlehem far away
   and laid in a manger of
   sweet-smelling hay.
Angels sang and the Wise men knew that
   Jesus would always love me and you.

God made me.
God made you.

He made goats,

sheep,

and camels too."

13

We are spinning the arrow
around once more.
After it stops, we'll knock
on a door.

"Let's be friends.
We'll stay to play.
Then we can tell you of
Jesus today.

15

"You play the drums,
and we'll sing you a song
about Little Lord Jesus . . .
as we hike along.

God loves all people,
and He made us all—
black, brown, or red—
short, big, or tall.
God made me. God made you.
He made the giraffe and
    the elephant too."

Spin the arrow
around once more.
We'll see where it stops.
Then we'll knock on a door.

We wave a greeting
as "Hi, friends," we say.
"We've come from our church...
though it's quite far away...
to tell you of Jesus
and His love today.

"Jesus loves us, this we know . . .
for the Bible tells us so.
The Bible is God's special Book.
We've brought you one.
Please come and look.

God made me.
God made you.

He made donkeys,

llamas,

and jaguars too."

Isn't this fun?
We'll spin the arrow once more.
Where do you think
we will knock on a door?

We wait for an answer.
Then, "Hi, friends," we say.
"We've come from our church.
It is quite far away.
We've come to tell you
    of Jesus today.

"To tell of His kindness . . .
His love and care . . .
for all of God's children
everywhere.

God made me,
God made you.

He made flowers,

cherry trees,

and the water too."

Here we are back,
and our game is all done.
Now wasn't it fun
to meet everyone?

Although we were playing,
we all know it's true . . .
telling of Jesus
is the thing we should do.

Children live in different houses.

They have different clothes
   to wear.
They have different colored
   eyes and skin,
and different kinds of hair.

They have different pets and games.

They eat different foods each day.

But the same God made each one—
each in a special way.

And each one needs to know Jesus . . .
needs to know His love and care.
Let's tell the story of Jesus.
Let's tell it everywhere!